My Phonics WORD BOOK

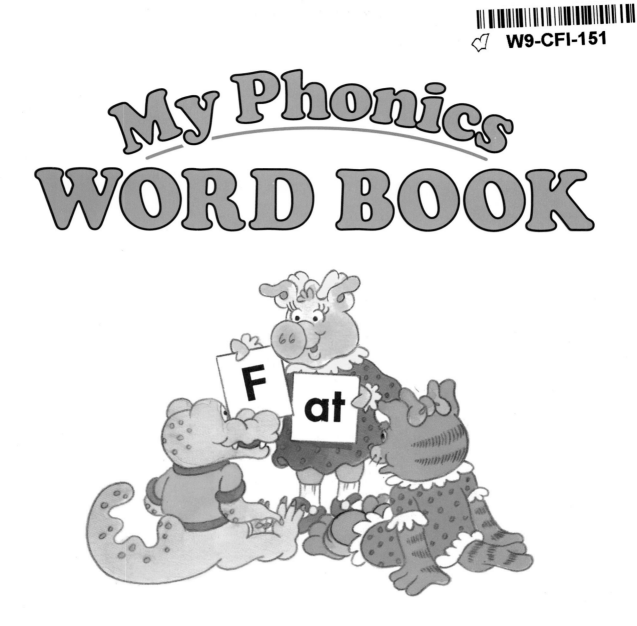

Written by Cass Hollander
Illustrated by Dick Morgado

Published by McClanahan Book Co., Inc. 23 West 26th St.
New York, NY 10010
Printed in the U.S.A.

bag

Pack a **bag.**

rag

Use a **rag.**

drag

Drag a bag.

tag

Playing **tag**

flag

Wave a **flag.**

wag

Tails that **wag**

am

clam
dam
ham
jam
slam
yam

clam

Dig a **clam.**

jam

Mmmm…mmm **jam**

dam

Make a **dam.**

slam

Don't let it **slam!**

ham

Bake a **ham.**

yam

YAMS

Pick a **yam.**

an

can
fan
man
pan
ran
van

can

Open a **can.**

pan
Wash a **pan.**

fan
Stop that **fan!**

ran
She ran and **ran.**

man
Meet a **man.**

van
I have a **van.**

cap

I love my **cap!**

map

Look at the **map.**

clap

Tap and **clap.**

nap

Take a **nap.**

lap

Sit on a **lap.**

strap

Fix the **strap.**

ar

bar
car
far
jar
star
tar

bar

Chocolate **bar**

jar

Pickle **jar**

car

Yellow **car**

star

Wish on a **star.**

far

Going **far**

tar

Stuck in **tar.**

bat

Swing a **bat.**

hat

Hold on to your **hat!**

cat

Pet a **cat.**

mat

Sweep the **mat.**

fat

Short and **fat**

sat

The cat just **sat.**

en

hen
men
pen
ten
then
when

hen

Get that **hen!**

ten

Count to **ten.**

men

Ten **men**

then

Now and **then**

pen

Pick a **pen.**

when

Say **when!**

et

get
jet
let
net
pet
wet

get

Get ready! Get set!

net

Jump the net.

jet

Fly a jet.

pet

Feed a pet.

let

Let me pet.

wet

Don't get wet!

ig

big
dig
jig
pig
twig
wig

big

So **big!**

pig

A pretty **pig!**

dig

Dig and **dig.**

twig

Use a **twig.**

jig

Dance a **jig.**

wig

What a **wig!**

in

chin
fin
pin
spin
twin
win

chin

My **chin chin chin**

spin

Tops **spin.**

fin

A purple **fin**

twin

Find the **twin.**

pin

Find a **pin.**

win

Who will **win?**

op

chop
hop
mop
pop
stop
top

chop

Chop, chop, chop!

pop

Pop!

hop

Hop, hop, hop!

stop

I can't **stop!**

mop

Dance with a **mop.**

top

Spin a **top.**

ot

got
hot
lot
not
pot
spot

got

What have you **got?**

not

Ready or **not!**

hot

Too **hot!**

pot

Oh no! The **pot!**

lot

Thanks a **lot!**

spot

A bad **spot**

OW

bow
chow
cow
how
now
plow

bow

Take a **bow.**

how

Find out **how.**

chow

Time for **chow!**

now

Come out **now!**

cow

Milk a **cow.**

plow

Pull a **plow.**

ub

club
cub
rub
scrub
shrub
tub

club

Be in the **club!**

scrub

Scrub and **scrub.**

cub

Hug a **cub.**

shrub

Plant a **shrub.**

rub

Pat. Don't **rub.**

tub

Duck in the **tub.**

bug

See a **bug.**

mug

This is my **mug.**

hug

A big **hug!**

rug

Sweep the **rug.**

jug

Fill the **jug.**

tug

Tug and **tug**

ail

mail
nail
pail
sail
snail
tail

mail

Get the **mail.**

sail

Put up the **sail.**

nail

Hammer a **nail.**

snail

Race a **snail.**

pail

Fill a **pail.**

tail

Wag a **tail.**

ain

brain
chain
plain
rain
stain
train

brain

Use your **brain.**

rain

Rain, rain, rain!

chain

Make a **chain.**

stain

Fix a **stain.**

plain

Fancy or **plain?**

train

Take a **train.**

ake

bake
cake
lake
rake
snake
take

bake

Time to **bake.**

rake

Drop the **rake.**

cake

I love **cake!**

snake

Oh, oh! A **snake!**

lake

Jump in the **lake.**

take

Take the cake.

all

ball
call
fall
hall
small
wall

ball

Play **ball.**

hall

Hide in the **hall.**

call

Make a **call.**

small

Make yourself **small.**

fall

Do not **fall.**

wall

Paint a **wall.**

ate

date
gate
late
plate
skate
state

date

What is the **date?**

plate

Dropped a **plate!**

gate

Open the **gate.**

skate

Fix a **skate.**

late

CLOSED

Too **late!**

state

UNITED STATES

Find your **state.**

eep

creep
deep
jeep
keep
sheep
sleep

- 42 -

creep

Caterpillars **creep.**

keep

Sell or **keep?**

deep

Dive down **deep.**

sheep

...4 ...5 ...6...

Counting **sheep**

jeep

Go in a **jeep.**

sleep

Go to **sleep.**

eet

beet
feet
greet
meet
sheet
street

beet

Pull up a **beet.**

meet

Did you **meet?**

feet

Tap your **feet.**

sheet

Fold a **sheet.**

greet

Meet and **greet.**

street

Cross a **street.**

ell

bell
fell
shell
smell
tell
well

bell

Ring the **bell.**

smell

What a **smell!**

fell

Who **fell?**

tell

Show and **tell.**

shell

Hide in your **shell.**

well

Go to the **well.**

est

best
nest
pest
rest
test
vest

best

Do your **best.**

rest

Sit and **rest.**

nest

Make a **nest.**

test

Take a **test.**

pest

What a **pest!**

vest

Button your **vest.**

ick

brick
chick
kick
lick
sick
stick

brick

Lay a **brick.**

lick

Lick and **lick!**

chick

A baby **chick**

sick

I feel **sick.**

kick

Make the **kick.**

stick

Get a **stick.**

ing

king
ring
sing
sting
string
swing

king

Meet a **king.**

sting

Bees can **sting!**

ring

Look at my **ring.**

string

Too much **string!**

sing

Dance and **sing.**

swing

Swing on a **swing.**

ink

drink
pink
rink
sink
think
wink

drink

Take a **drink.**

sink

Dishes in the **sink**

pink

Paint it **pink.**

think

Sit and **think.**

rink

Skate in the **rink.**

wink

Smile and **wink.**

ock

block
clock
dock
lock
rock
sock

block

Add a **block.**

lock

Open the **lock.**

clock

Set the **clock.**

rock

Find a **rock.**

dock

Step on the **dock.**

sock

Oh, no! My **sock!**

ook

book
brook
cook
hook
look
shook

book

I like my **book.**

hook

Use the **hook!**

brook

Fall in the **brook.**

look

Take a **look.**

cook

Cook, cook, cook!

shook

He **shook** and **shook!**

own

brown
clown
crown
down
frown
town

brown

Chocolate is **brown.**

down

Don't look **down!**

clown

Dance with a **clown.**

frown

Smile! Don't **frown!**

crown

Put on a **crown.**

town

Go to **town.**

ark

bark
dark
mark
park
shark
spark

art

cart
dart
part
smart
start
tart

bark

They all **bark!**

park

In the **park**

dark

It's very **dark.**

shark

Meet a **shark.**

mark

Make a **mark.**

spark

See a **spark.**

cart

Push a **cart.**

tart

Eat a **tart.**

dart

Look out for the **dart.**

smart

Get **smart.**

part

Play a **part.**

start

When does it **start?**

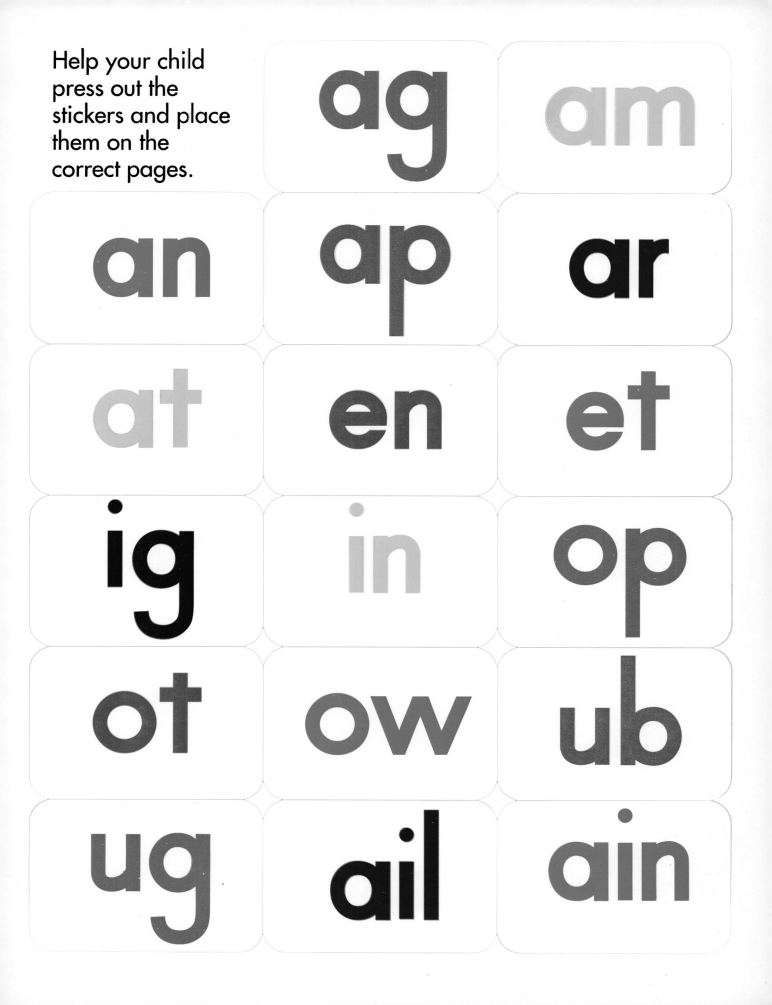

Help your child press out the stickers and place them on the correct pages.

ag

am

an

ap

ar

at

en

et

ig

in

op

ot

ow

ub

ug

ail

ain